Whispers of
Horse Island

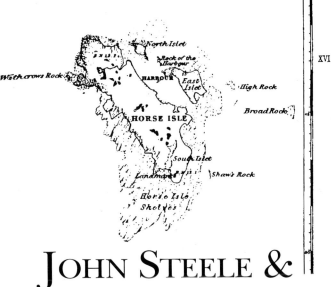

XVI

JOHN STEELE &
NOREEN STEELE

Argyll

publishing

© John Steele & Noreen Steele 1999

First published 1999
Argyll Publishing
Glendaruel
Argyll PA22 3AE
Scotland

The authors have asserted their moral rights.

British Library Cataloguing-in-Publication Data.

**A catalogue record for this book is available from the
British Library.**

ISBN 1 902831 05 5

Origination Cordfall Ltd, Glasgow

Printing ColourBooks Ltd, Dublin

To our delightful grandchildren
Rob, Kirsten, Campbell,
Blair, Findlay, Sally and Harrison

CONTENTS

HORSE ISLAND – THE NAME

The Firth of Clyde on the west coast of Scotland has always been a top Scottish holiday destination. The islands of Arran, Bute and Cumbrae are particularly easy to reach due to the frequent ferry crossings and excellent train services to the ferry terminals. The Island of Arran is by far the largest and busiest of the islands. Each year Caledonian MacBrayne's impressive car ferry *Caledonian Isles* carries in excess of six hundred thousand passengers between Ardrossan and Brodick. As the Arran ferry departs from Ardrossan the panoramic view is splendid with the prominent rock of Ailsa Craig protruding majestically in the distance. Half a mile from Ardrossan Harbour the *Caledonian Isles* slips past Horse Island. Viewed from the mainland the island appears as a long narrow strip. With the benefit of height from the deck of the ship the true shape and size of the island can be seen sprawling outwards. There are no trees but it has a dense covering of grass and wild flowers. Almost its entire coastline is rocky with treacherous submerged shelves and outlying rocks. One small sandy bay is situated on the leeward side. A conspicuous stone-built tower stands at the southern tip of the island. Horse Island is low-lying and is frequently covered by the stormy sea leaving only the tower to mark its presence.

Horse Island is an intriguing name and there are a number of local explanations as to its origin. Could there have been horses on it? There is a local legend that horses were taken out to the island and left to graze. In fact it was cattle that were taken out from Montfode Farm on the North Shore of Ardrossan. The cattle were driven down to the beach

There are no trees on Horse Island but it has a dense covering of grass and wild flowers mainly white Marguerette daisies and mauve Michaelmas daisies

where they were walked out, at low tide. An open boat then led the way across the channel with the cattle swimming behind. Herds were guided into the small sandy bay where they could walk easily ashore and were left to wander unhindered and graze undisturbed on the lush green grass.

Another local story put forward for the name was that a ship had been wrecked and horses had managed to swim onto the island and save themselves from drowning. Intensive research has shown nothing to substantiate this theory.

It is also told locally that when horses were imported from Ireland they were put ashore on the island before reaching the mainland in an attempt to avoid paying import tax. No written proof has been found to validate this.

Some people are of the belief that the name was acquired because the outline of the island resembles the shape of a horse. When viewed from a low flying aircraft this speculation is disproved as there is no likeness whatsoever. Another local theory, that could not be traced, is that the island was named after a Captain Horse who was once stranded there.

To trace the origin of the name, we must go back to the twelfth century, to the reign of King David I of Scotland (1124–1153). The King encouraged Richard de Morville from Huntingdon in the Kingdom of England, to settle in Scotland and rewarded him with huge grants of land in Lothian and Lauderdale and in Ayrshire. He was appointed Great Constable of Scotland and also Lord of Cunninghame

The first view of Horse Island on leaving the harbour at Ardrossan

John Coleman

and Largs. Richard de Morville founded a most impressive abbey at Kilwinning in north Ayrshire, *circa* 1140. The abbey was occupied by an Abbot and Prior who oversaw a group of Benedictine Monks. (De Morville became a monk before his death in 1162.) He ruled Cunninghame well and was a popular leader with numerous loyal followers. As a reward for their allegiance to him they were each given grants of land as was the custom. In Cunninghame many gifts of land were bestowed upon his faithful vassals.

One of the main recipients was Philip de Horssey who was married to de Morville's daughter Dorothea. Philip de Horssey was given land which included the valuable estate of Warrix in the Parish of Dreghorn, nine miles south of Ardrossan. He inherited the small island, comprising of about twelve acres, situated half a mile from the North Shore of Ardrossan. The island was thereafter referred to as Horssey's Island. Through the passage of time the name evolved into Horse Island.

Herring gulls and Lesser Black-backed gulls have become the dominant species on Horse Island

John Coleman

CHANGES TO NUMBERS OF BREEDING TERN ON HORSE ISLAND				
Year	Common Tern	Arctic Tern	Sandwich Tern	Roseate Tern
1961	c200	c200	c185	c20
1970	150	150	0	11
1975	c85	c56	+57	0
1980	116	58	0	0
1985	0	0	0	0
1990	0	0	0	0
1999	0	0	0	0

A HAVEN FOR BIRDS

Horse Island has always been a safe haven for wild birds. Although small, its varying habitat caters to the needs of the different breeds. The middle of the island is thickly covered in rich, tall vegetation, which offers some protection from the wind and rain and also cover from the larger predatory birds. Numerous pools of deep water lie hidden amid the high undergrowth and offer perfect breeding conditions for the moorhen that sometimes nest there.

During the early 1960s a growing number of four species of Tern returned each summer. Sandwich Tern, Arctic Tern, Common Tern and the rare Roseate Tern. The first to arrive being almost two hundred pairs of Sandwich Tern. Next to arrive in the same numbers were the Common and Arctic Tern. By June about twenty pairs of Roseate Tern would have formed a colony in the centre of the island.

Due to local activity, most notably by Gordon Fraser, the Royal Society for the Protection of Birds showed a keen interest in Horse Island from the 1950s. This was mainly due to the large number of Tern, including Arctic Tern, nesting there. In 1961 the Ardrossan Harbour Company, the owner of the island, agreed informally that the RSPB should be in charge of the management of Horse Island for the protection of wild birds and their environment.

The Secretary of State for Scotland granted the RSPB's request that Horse Island be designated a bird sanctuary and the Wild Birds (Horse Island Sanctuary) Order 1963 came into effect on 1st March that year. This means that it is an offence to attempt to kill, injure or take any bird or to

Eider Duck on nest

Ian Fraser & Gordon Fraser

Ringed Plover at nest

steal or destroy any wild birds' eggs. Access on to Horse Island is allowed only with the written authority of the RSPB. Under the Wildlife and Countryside Act Horse Island is designated an Area of Special Protection.

Sadly the number of breeding Tern has declined dramatically with only occasional breeding by a few pairs in recent years. In comparison there has been a steady and significant increase in the number of Herring and Lesser Black-backed Gulls on the island.

Sandwich Tern on guard duty

Oystercatcher at nest with Terns behind

    The RSPB undertakes an annual census of the breeding birds on the island. On 21st May 1998, a team of five observers, Jim Tod, Zul Bhatia, Douglas Barr, David Eadie and Chris Waltho were taken across from Ardrossan by boatmen Alex Kelly and Bill McKnight. During a census the main part of the island is counted in fourteen parallel sections with the five observers walking side by side (at the same pace) on a broad front recording all nests found. Counting of the main island starts at the tower end and finishes at the rocky headland in the north. The edges of each section are marked with a line of bamboo canes each with a conspicuous red flag on top. The five observers thoroughly cover the whole island by walking about fifteen feet (4.5 metres) apart from each other and count nests on either side of them. Double counting is avoided by adjacent observers keeping each other briefed on what has already been counted.

On this most recent occasion it would have been too time-consuming to record clutch sizes of all the nests and, except for some of the Eider (the object of a special study by Chris Waltho, one of the observers) and the Cormorant, this was not done. A total of 2,897 nests were recorded, the most numerous being the Lesser Black-backed Gull and the Herring Gull.

The Cormorant is a recent coloniser of the island with the first nest recorded in 1966. The following year there were sixteen nests. During this 1998 census thirty nine nests were found in one colony on East Islet. Three of the nests were empty (probably yet to lay?).

There were two Mute Swan nests, both of which were being incubated. One contained five eggs and the other incubating bird sat tight. No effort was made to put her off the nest. Four immature birds were present on the sandy/muddy bay near the East Islet.

One Greylag was incubating five eggs. This would appear to be the first breeding record on the island.

A Barnacle Goose was incubating five eggs. Its mate was standing nearby. Both were 'pure' Barnacles. This would appear to be the first breeding record for the island, although in 1997 the observers recorded "a very vocal and territorial pair" but no nest was found that year.

The 440 Eider nests counted was probably a slight underestimate as some nests had chicks and earlier ones would have left the area. Some birds also sat very tight and the observers could easily have passed by close to the nest without realising it was there. Breeding Eider have increased very significantly on Horse Island with an average of 424 nests per year during 1994–1998 compared to 244 for the

Greater Black Backed Gull

Ian Fraser & Gordon Fraser

period 1989–1993. They have also shown a similar increase throughout the whole Clyde area.

Although only three Oystercatcher nests were found, it was likely that some were overlooked as there were many birds around including a flock of twelve on a tiny islet. Three Dunlin in full breeding plumage were at a pool on the main island. An estimated three pairs of Rockpit were present, food carrying being observed. It is possible that two Crows were nesting in the tower. Three Shelduck were present on the sandy/muddy bay. A single Mallard was seen.

Since the RSPB became responsible for managing Horse Island the birds have been left undisturbed. It is essential that this remains so as the island is small and the breeding sites are extensive. It is forbidden to visit the island during the breeding season. Written permission from the RSPB must be obtained at all times before an intended visit. In any case, the island is situated close to the shore and this offers an ideal bird watching location.

Further information regarding Horse Island Bird Sanctuary can be obtained from the RSPB Nature Reserve at Lochwinnoch 01505 842663.

Information regarding the RSPB can be obtained from the Scottish Headquarters. Dunedin House, 25 Ravelston Terrace, Edinburgh. Tel 0131 311 6500 or the UK Headquarters at The Lodge, Sandy, Bedfordshire SG19 2DL. Tel 01767 680551.

Eggs of Ringed Plover

Ian Fraser & Gordon Fraser

Ian Fraser & Gordon Fraser

Black Headed Gull chick at point of hatch

Ian Fraser & Gordon Fraser

Herring Gull nest

Herring Gull nest

Resting Cormorants

John Robertson

Ian Fraser & Gordon Fraser

Tony Barr

The port of Ardrossan in the days of sailing ships –
the Earl of Eglinton's plan to make Ardrossan
the major port on the Clyde led to the building of Ardrossan harbour

THE EARL'S VISION

Hugh, 12th Earl of Eglinton (1739 – 1819) was an exceedingly wealthy nobleman who owned vast prosperous estates in Ayrshire. He had great vision for the future and was intent on establishing Ardrossan as the principal sea port for the south west of Scotland. He became dedicated to this cause and invested an immense amount of his own money and time towards attaining his objective. In 1805 the Earl obtained an Act of Parliament to allow the construction of a grand harbour at Ardrossan. The Act read,

Erecting And Maintaining A Harbour, Docks And Other Works, At Ardrossan.[1]

Where there is a promontory or point called Ardrossan in the Parish of Ardrossan, in the County of Ayr, terminated by a ridge of rocks stretching for a considerable way into the sea in a north west direction. Immediately opposite to which at the distance of about half a mile to the north west, there is an island called Horse Island.

The distinguished engineer Thomas Telford carried out the initial survey work and drew up elaborate plans for the ambitious project. The following year almost two hundred men were given regular employment in the construction of the harbour. The workforce comprised twenty-one masons, thirty-five quarry men, five smiths, seven wrights and over one hundred labourers.

---

1. Ardrossan as a place name is derived from *ard*: a height, *ross*: a point or promontory, *an*: a diminutive.

Incorporated in the grand plan was a proposal to link Ardrossan with Glasgow via the construction of a canal. The planned canal, thirty three miles in length, would enable the speedy transportation of goods between the Port of Ardrossan and the City of Glasgow. The River Clyde was undredged at this time and presented a slow hazardous journey to the vast number of sailing ships vying for this route to Glasgow.

Thomas Telford also perceived that Horse Island could be put to good use as a natural shelter with the addition of two extending breakwater walls being built out from the island – to protect the harbour from the north winds and against the prevailing south westerlies. This futuristic plan was later decided against and unfortunately work never started.

A contemporary of the Earl of Eglinton was the world famous John Ross, renowned Arctic explorer. John Ross was greatly concerned about the dangers Horse Island presented to the increasing number of sailing ships entering the harbour. The island stands only a few feet in height and during the harsh winter storms the sea surges over the entire island completely submerging it. Ship captains unfamiliar with the area could be completely unaware of the terrible dangers lurking under the shallow covering of water. If the wooden-built vessels did not steer well clear of the island and its widespread rocks they would be sailing to their doom.

John Ross advised strongly that a tall beacon tower be constructed on the most southern tip of the island as a navigation warning to the location of the hazards. The tower would also serve as a refuge to any unfortunate mariners who came to be stranded on the island after their ship foundered on the rocks.

Thankfully the advice of this experienced Arctic seafarer was heeded and a conspicuous white, stone beacon tower was constructed in the year 1811. The square tower was built fifty two feet (15.8 metres) in height with three windows on each side.

John Ross was later knighted and went on to become a Rear Admiral.

The engineer Thomas Telford prepared this plan to build breakwaters extending from Horse Island to provide shelter for the new harbour – a plan never realised

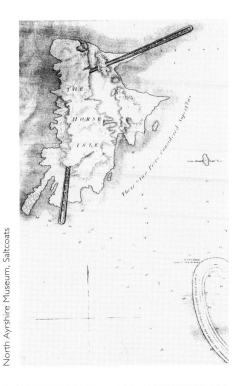

North Ayrshire Museum, Saltcoats

Work in progress on the new Ardrossan harbour around 1887

Tony Barr

John Robertson

John Ross, the Arctic explorer, advised that a
warning beacon tower be built on Horse Island
to warn shipping of the danger – his advice was
heeded and a white, stone beacon tower 52 feet
in height was constructed in 1811

Tony Barr

During the construction of the harbour the building of the Glasgow, Paisley and Ardrossan Canal progressed without hindrance and promised easy passage to the City of Glasgow for the import and export of goods from the trading vessels arriving at Ardrossan.

As work neared completion on the stretch of the canal between Paisley and Johnstone a specially designed canal boat, known as a fly boat, had been commissioned to ply the water way. This vessel was launched in Paisley on 31st October 1810 and named *Countess of Eglinton*. It was sixty feet (18 metres) in length, eight feet (2.4 metres) wide and designed to carry one hundred and fifty passengers. An enclosed cabin provided comfort for the first and second class passengers, the roof of which served as an upper open deck.

On November 6th this section of the canal was declared open and the canal boat set off on its four mile maiden journey pulled along by two strong horses at a speed of three miles per hour. It was a pleasant mode of transport. Until now the only means of travel between the two towns had been provided by the uncomfortable once weekly stage coach.

The Member of Parliament for the area the Right Honourable Archibald Speirs lived in the village of Elderslie between Paisley and Johnstone. He specialised in this new form of transport, having visited many canals throughout Britain and was an acknowledged expert in canal boats.

Archibald Speirs was very critical of the newly built vessel and stated strongly that it was completely unsuitable and unsafe. The distinguished gentleman's opinion went unheeded and unfortunately he was soon proved right. Only four days after the grand ceremony declaring this section of the canal open, a terrible tragedy took place. There was great excitement in Paisley as Saturday 10th November was the annual Martinmas Fair, one of the few days in the year when all the factories and thread mills closed for a one day holiday. Hundreds of Paisley 'Buddies' with their families, all dressed in their Sunday best, congregated at the Paisley Basin where the *Countess of Eglinton* would berth to allow the passengers travelling from Johnstone to disembark. The waiting crowd was eagerly anticipating an enjoyable leisurely boat trip to Johnstone. When the canal boat came into view it was fully laden with Johnstone folk.

As the vessel came to a halt the over-excited crowd surged forward. For many of them this would be their very first time on a boat. As the passengers tried to step from the vessel on to the embankment they were being jostled by the unruly Paisley throng swarming on board. It was obvious to all that the waiting numbers far exceeded the passenger capacity of the vessel.

The two concerned boatmen tried to bring some order to the chaos but stood no chance and things quickly got out of control. The fact that the fly boat was on a level height with the embankment added to the pandemonium as this enabled the would-be passengers to scramble aboard using the full length of the boat.

It was a sunny day and on boarding the majority tried to reach the top open deck. With so many people trying to board and the Johnstone passengers attempting to get off, the vessel slowly tilted over. The two boatmen reacted very quickly and tried to push the vessel away from the embankment to ensure that no one else could board the already overloaded boat. The frenzied crowd on the banks were having none of this and began to leap frantically on board.

The two anxious crewmen were making progress in

The beacon tower on Horse Island shown against the Arran hills

An early picture of Ardrossan Harbour looking out to Horse Island

John Coleman

North Ayrshire Museum, Saltcoats

pushing the boat away from the embankment and the widening gap ensured that no one else could jump on. But by now far too many people had scrambled onto the canal boat making it dangerously unstable. Too many passengers were now on the upper deck and the fly boat became top heavy. With the edge of the embankment no longer assisting the stability of the vessel, it capsized pitching everyone on the outer deck into the water. Suddenly a happy outing had become a nightmare. The passengers trapped inside the cabin had little chance of escape and most lost their lives. On the embankment the two frightened horses were released from their ropes and bolted. Within minutes eighty-five people had drowned, trapped in the confined canal basin. The youngest victim was a baby girl of only six months.

After this terrible disaster, interest in the canal as a means of transport diminished as it had been the cause of great distress to so many people. With the lack of public confidence, unforeseen rising costs and the withdrawal of financial support from the shareholders, the canal project was completely abandoned one year after the disaster with a loss of £71,000.

The Earl of Eglinton, who was now also Lord Ardrossan ensured the construction of the harbour continued until his death in 1819 when work was suspended. The building work recommenced after six years and coincided with the opening of a shipyard within the harbour.

As the Earl had visualised, Ardrossan did develop into a major port bringing much prosperity to the district. North Ayrshire became a heavily industrialised area with thriving coal mines easily accessible. By 1840 Ardrossan was exporting in excess of 60,000 tons of coal annually. The dock workers were kept in full employment handling the continual arrival and departure of vessels carrying general cargo. The Earl's vision had most certainly materialized.

With its hidden shelves and treacherous rocks, Horse Island has been a graveyard for many a ship using Ardrossan Harbour – evidence of wrecks is extensive, including hulks like the one above, parts of ships and signs of lost cargoes such as coal

SHIPWRECKS AND SORROWS

Since the time when the level of trade at Ardrossan Harbour really took off, Horse Island has been the cause of much despair and death. Many a ship has come to grief after being blown onto the razor sharp rocks and hidden shelves surrounding the island. And after a ship had foundered on the rocks it was soon smashed to pieces by the relentless pounding of the storm-tossed waves.

The need for a lifeboat became apparent with the ever increasing number of trading vessels calling at the harbour. In 1820 a short range harbour lifeboat was gifted to Ardrossan.

The lifeboat proved its worth in 1830 when it was summoned to render assistance when the Saltcoats registered collier brig *Lady Montgomerie* was seen to be in severe distress.

The rescue crew consisting of ten local volunteers launched the lifeboat in the most appalling sea conditions. Great strength and skill were required to man the oars in a brave attempt to reach the vessel which was being swamped by enormous waves and in great danger of being grounded on Horse Island.

As the captain of the *Lady Montgomerie* fought to keep control of his brig a huge wave washed him overboard along with two crewmen. The two young apprentices who were on board watched horrified as the three men disappeared into the angry sea. The two boys were left alone clinging desperately to the deck trying to save themselves from the same fate.

On reaching the scene the lifeboat crew struggled to hold their boat alongside the stricken vessel. The brave lifeboat men risked their lives in an attempt to rescue the stranded youngsters. Both boys were successfully lifted into the lifeboat which then faced a terrible journey back to the harbour in difficult turbulent conditions.

During October 1860 a small cargo vessel was heading for Ardrossan Harbour. Unfortunately the skipper had set his course too close to Horse Island and his ship ran aground on the notorious submerged shelves. The island had claimed another victim. Luckily for the stranded crew help was soon in coming. A Saltcoats fishing boat was nearby and quickly came to the rescue. The fishermen, with their local knowledge, were able to navigate round the rocks and rescue the crew before any harm came to them. Ardrossan businessmen raised a sum of money to reward the brave fishermen. A presentation was arranged and Alex Mathison accepted the money on behalf of his fellow rescuers from local shipbuilder Joseph Russell.

During December 1869 a local vessel, on returning to Ardrossan, informed the harbour authorities that they had sighted a small sailing ship at a position one and a half miles out to sea. The vessel appeared to be water logged and drifting on a course which would ground her on Horse Island.

The following day a water cask floated ashore at Ardrossan. Four local men, Thomas Harvey, John Blue, Robert Currie and James McPhee were so concerned about the safety of the crew from the sailing ship that they rowed over to Horse Island to search for them. On reaching the island the men came upon some wreckage which included a cargo hatch, gangway hand rail, a few bulwark boards and a large quantity of carrots were floating about. On the beach was a ship's small clinker-built boat twelve feet long (3.6 metres). There was no name painted on the boat to identify the wrecked sailing ship and no bodies were ever recovered.

The Ardrossan lifeboat could only render assistance in the vicinity of the harbour. It was of no use for rescues further out in the open sea. The short range lifeboat could offer no assistance to the twenty passengers and crew of the *City of Edinburgh*, an iron vessel built in Glasgow, when it ran aground on Ailsa Craig, in the Firth of Clyde, during the month of January 1870.

This incident proved the urgent need for a suitable lifeboat to cover all of the Firth of Clyde, including Bute and the Cumbraes. The provost and councillors of Ardrossan joined forces with the harbour authorities to appeal to the Royal National Lifeboat Institution to supply a suitable boat based at Ardrossan. Six months later a lifeboat station was opened in Ardrossan and a new self-righting lifeboat, the *Fair Maid of Perth* allocated to it. This new rowing boat had ten oars double banked and had just been constructed at a cost of £234.

Not long after, on January 1st 1871, the brig, *Morning Star* of Dublin was seen to be struggling through a strong south westerly gale trying to reach the sanctuary of Ardrossan Harbour. The residents of the harbour houses watched as the vessel battled against the elements and they became increasingly concerned as the strong tides swept the one hundred and seventy ton Dutch-built brig off course. The *Morning Star*, owned by Mr J Dalargy of Dublin, was quite accustomed to coasting around the waters of the Clyde and was well-known in the area.

As the strong winds and currents drove her towards the rocks lying off the north west of Horse Island the locals raced to alert the lifeboat crew.

Before the gun could be fired, which summoned the crew to man the lifeboat, the ill-fated *Morning Star* crashed onto the rocks and broke up on impact. Parts of the wreckage were carried away by the fierce winds and waves. The six badly shocked crew members were left clinging to the rocks that had claimed their ship. Although Horse Island was close by, the survivors could not attempt to reach it as all their strength was required to maintain a hold on the rocks against the force of the freezing waves lashing over them.

As they approached the wreck the lifeboat men realised it was impossible to get close enough to rescue the shipwrecked mariners without the lifeboat also being swept onto the rocks. The lifeboat coxswain quickly sought the assistance of the harbour tug which towed them to the sheltered side of Horse Island. On reaching a place where they could beach the *Fair Maid of Perth* some of the lifeboat crew were landed. With great difficulty they scrambled across the island, hampered by the heavy rescue ropes they were carrying. The rescuers made slow progress as the harsh wind and rain hurled against them. The lifeboat crew got as near as possible then threw the ropes to the exhausted men stranded on the rocks and one by one they were dragged through the turbulent channel onto the island. The six man crew of the *Morning Star* all survived this terrible ordeal and were helped back to the waiting lifeboat then ferried safely to Ardrossan Harbour.

The most serious shipping disaster ever witnessed in Ardrossan took place on 21st October 1874. The vessel involved was the 1381 gross ton iron paddle steamer *Chusan*, built in the Clyde by John Elder and Son, Govan. Second-hand engines from America had been fitted to the paddle steamer which was 300 feet long (91 metres) and 50 feet wide (15 metres). The vessel was owned by the China Steam Navigation Company of Shanghai and intended for trading in the Yangtze River. It was registered in the name of Charles Lloyd Norman who was the British agent for the company. The *Chusan* had been launched only the previous month in September 1874.

The paddle steamer departed on her maiden voyage from the Clyde, on October 8th 1874, bound for the Yangtze River, via Waterford in Ireland, then Suez and Singapore. In command was American Captain George C Johnstone, accompanied by his pregnant wife and their four year-old son George. His wife's sister Miss Helen Elliot was sailing as a stewardess. Also on board was Mr May, the engineer who had supervised the construction of the vessel and a Mr Moir, a registered Clyde River and Estuary pilot. Mr Moir lived in Greenock and had been a pilot for one year. Captain King travelling as a passenger was aboard to gain experience of

The paddle steamer *Chusan* came to grief on Horse Island
rocks in 1874 with serious loss of life

this type of vessel as he was taking command of a sister ship
the *Kiang Loongs* which was being built at Govan also. The
senior crew members were the ship's first mate John Murdoch
Johnstone, from Glasgow (no relation to the captain), William
Miller 2nd mate from Fort William, William Gardiner chief
engineer from Leith, William Ortwin 2nd engineer from
Liverpool, William Wrench 3rd engineer from Abernethy,
George Marr 4th engineer from Aberdeen and Purser
Edward Humphries from Salem, Massachusetts. The
remainder of the crew were of West African, South American,
Asian and West Indies origin. Sixteen were employed as
firemen, to shovel the vast amount of coal used to fire the
boilers. The rest comprised two cooks, three stewards and
eighteen seamen.

During the *Chusan*'s maiden voyage from the River Clyde
serious defects were detected in the riveting and plating.
On arrival at Waterford, Ireland Mr May, Captain King and

the pilot, Captain Johnstone contacted the ship's owners to report the defects. The owners' insurance underwriters the Maritime Insurance Company immediately contacted Captain Lodge, an eminent ship's surveyor, to examine the paddle steamer to ascertain if the ship was in a fit condition to return to Glasgow. He surveyed the ship but saw nothing which led him to believe that the vessel should not return to the Clyde. The paddle steamer could have been repaired at Waterford but he considered it extremely unwise for a vessel like the *Chusan* to embark on a long voyage to China during the month of October. As the paddle steamer was now returning to Glasgow Mr May, Mr Moir the pilot and Captain King remained on board.

On the evening of 20th October 1874 the *Chusan* set off on her return voyage in fine weather conditions. After leaving the shelter of the Belfast Lough Captain Johnstone became concerned by the sudden deterioration of the weather. By 2am the paddle steamer had reached Ailsa Craig in the Firth of Clyde when a sudden violent storm blew up. It was so severe the vessel's course was changed to seek the shelter of Pladda Isle at the southern tip of the Isle of Arran.

The captain fought a desperate battle against the stormy sea throughout the night. When the gale force winds hit the *Chusan* broadsides one paddle would dip as the other lifted out of the water making it almost impossible to steer. With the firemen furiously fuelling the boilers the stock of coal was diminishing quickly making the *Chusan* lighter in the water and more liable to be tossed around by the heavy swell.

On approaching Pladda the vessel was not responding well to steering. The engine speed was reduced considerably in an attempt to maintain control of the paddle steamer. The situation became so desperate they now battled on through the terrible storm, towards Holy Isle hoping to gain shelter in Lamlash Bay.

The strength of the gale force wind was still increasing and the vessel was being damaged further. The two captains agreed it would be prudent to turn and make for Ardrossan. It would be risky but the Clyde pilot Mr Moir was familiar with the narrow harbour entrance and it seemed Captain

Johnstone had no other option. He was thankful to have the pilot still aboard.

As the *Chusan* changed course she was shown no mercy by the storm. Icy sheets of rain continuously swept across the decks as she ploughed her way slowly through the darkness, across the Clyde Estuary.

At 5am the welcome glare from Ardeer Iron Works in Stevenston, Ayrshire became visible. As the paddle steamer approached the harbour entrance the ship's captain took a bearing from the beacon tower on Horse Island. Meanwhile the lookout in the harbour pilot house became very concerned for the safety of the vessel and those on board. He quickly contacted Captain Archibald Steele, the Harbour Master, to advise him of the grave situation. Captain Steele alerted the berthing crew who were already on stand-by for the arrival of a Belfast steamer. The residents of the harbour houses gathered to watch the drama. As the small crowd huddled together they could see the *Chusan* rocking violently from side to side. Every time the vessel dipped over one of the huge 34 feet high (10 metres) paddle wheels came clear out of the water, churning furiously in the air.

On board the stricken vessel everyone was clinging for dear life as the pilot successfully navigated the paddle steamer within 200 yards (61 metres) of the harbour entrance. Suddenly a blast from the storm force wind slammed, with such terrible force, into the immense paddle boxes that the *Chusan* was pushed backwards completely out of control. The people on the quayside watched in horror as the paddle steamer was driven towards the cluster of rocks near Horse Island. With one almighty crash the vessel shuddered to a halt as it smashed against the rocks. The watching crowd were stunned to hear a loud crunch and see the paddle steamer snap completely in two. The stern section was held fast on the rocks. The forward section stayed afloat and was carried towards the harbour, where it struck against the pier. On impact two of the crew seized their chance and leapt to safety. A third man tried to follow but a moment's hesitation cost him his life as he tumbled into the widening gap and was swallowed by the waves. Other survivors were clinging on to a piece of wreckage, which was floating towards the harbour.

Meantime the other half of the paddle steamer was still stranded on the rocks with the remaining crew and passengers clutching at anything that would stop them from being washed overboard. The fierce wind howled as wave after wave swept over them. Weakened by the freezing cold and the terrible pounding of the waves Captain Johnstone's wife could hold on no longer and was dragged overboard. Without hesitation the captain jumped into the water grabbed his wife and held her afloat until she was hauled back on board. As an outstretched hand reached out to Captain Johnstone he slipped beneath the waves and was lost. Mrs Johnstone was no sooner back on board when her son George lost his grip and slid across the deck. The ship's purser, Ed Humphries, managed to catch the boy and hold him firmly, much to the relief of his distressed mother.

At Ardrossan as there was a delay in launching the lifeboat, four local men launched a small eighteen feet (5.5 metres) skiff in a desperate bid to save the men still clinging to the piece of wreckage. Their brave efforts were in vain as by the time they had rowed to the area there was no sign of survivors. The small boat then battled its way out to the wreck still stuck fast on the rocks where they made several gallant but unsuccessful attempts to come close. As their small skiff was in danger of being swamped they had to return reluctantly to the harbour.

Then a local tug under the command of Captain Bannatyne put to sea in this most atrocious weather. The valiant crew of the tug managed to save nine lives, including Chief Engineer William Gardiner and 2nd Engineer William Orton.

By now the lifeboat had been launched. In the difficult turbulent conditions second coxswain Henry Lipscombe positioned the lifeboat perilously close to the wreck. His fearless crew managed to haul on board the captain's son, Miss Elliot, John Johnstone the ship's mate and another three people. The rescue operation continued until 9am when all hope of finding more survivors was abandoned.

A few days later Captain Johnstone's body was washed ashore on the beach at North Crescent, Ardrossan. No trace of William Miller who had been washed overboard was ever found. His sea chest was recovered on the beach. Of the fifty two passengers and crew nine had lost their lives.

After the wreck of the Chusan on Horse Island with the loss of nine lives, a memorial was raised by public subscription and erected in Ardrossan Cemetery

The town was much saddened by this terrible disaster that had taken place in their midst. A large sum of money was raised, by public subscription, for the erection of a most prominent headstone in the local cemetery.

Five months after the disaster the *Chusan*'s sister vessel *Kiang Loongs* was launched in the Clyde, then dismantled and shipped in sections to China.

Most Saturdays found the local 'pier head skippers' strolling in the vicinity of the harbour, voicing their opinions on the various vessels busily coming and going, plying their trade. One Saturday afternoon during April 1879 a fairly fresh wind was blowing making the sea conditions extremely choppy. Around 2pm three 'pier head skippers' watched as the thirty two ton iron steamship *Moonlight* slipped out of the harbour. She was heavily laden with coal and heading up the Clyde estuary, on a short journey to Kirn near Dunoon.

One of the locals remarked to his two friends, "She might do to ferry over a mill pond but is hardly suitable for a voyage in the Clyde."

When the *Moonlight* left the confines of the harbour she started rolling erratically in the swelling sea. As the overloaded vessel dipped from side to side in the breaking waves water flooded down into the engine room. A thick pall of steam was seen to rise from the vessel as she slowly began to sink by the stern. Two crew members hurriedly swung out the small boat and jumped aboard. As they were just about to cast off from the sinking steamship the engineer appeared from below deck. With no time to spare he was hauled on board. Only a few seconds later their vessel disappeared beneath the waves.

Although Horse Island was close by the mariners had extreme difficulty in finding a safe passage through the razor sharp rocks. The three men were badly cut and bruised as they clambered over the jagged slippery rocks desperately trying to get on to the island.

By now the harbour tug and pilot boat had joined forces to rescue the stranded seamen and successfully managed to take all three on board. As the thankful sailors were rescued one of them, Captain Weir dismally stated that the *Moonlight* had not been insured.

The top of the mast was still to be seen on the following Wednesday. Two vessels with salvage experts from Greenock anchored beside the sunken steamer and pumped the *Moonlight* out. She slowly rose to the surface and was secured to the tug. As she was being towed to Ardrossan Harbour the steamer took in water and commenced to sink again. The crew on the salvage tug quickly cut the tow rope as their own vessel was now in immediate danger. No sooner had they severed the tow rope than the *Moonlight* disappeared beneath the waves once more. When the second sinking of the small steamer was reported to the salvage experts' headquarters in Greenock, it was decided that no more could be done and the vessel was given up as lost.

In 1880 the *Matilda Hillyards* a 589-ton barque was approaching Ardrossan on the last leg of her journey from Dieppe. The weather was worsening and a fierce south westerly gale was causing great concern to the ship's master John Anderson who ordered the ship's lights to be flashed to signal that assistance might be required.

This was also a signal to the local townsfolk to gather at the harbour to watch another drama unfold.

The harbour master instructed that the crew of the tug *Terrier* be put on stand-by ready to render assistance. By midnight the *Matilda Hillyards* was making slow but steady progress through the storm. The master was fearful that the strong south westerly wind would drive his vessel on to the perilous submerged rocks of Horse Island. As the *Matilda Hillyards* approached the harbour entrance she was caught in the grip of the storm and swept towards the island. The captain and crew were left helpless to prevent the barque careering out of control. The vessel slammed against the brutal rocks with such impact that both the main and fore masts snapped off completely.

The Ardrossan lifeboat was quickly launched with a full crew of volunteers, under the command of Coxswain Breckenridge. The men struggled against the storm pulling hard on the oars to reach the stricken vessel. As it was impossible to effect a rescue from the seaward side, the coxswain skilfully sailed the lifeboat to the sheltered side of Horse Island and landed his craft on the small beach, as he had done during previous rescues. The lifeboat crew then dragged all their heavy rescue equipment to the other side of the island. After three failed attempts they managed to secure rescue lines on to the stranded barque. The cold winter sea was washing over the twelve beleaguered seamen clinging on for dear life, to what remained of their ship.

As the storm raged the lifeboat crew managed to haul all the men through the surf one by one from the wreck. The rescuers had to almost carry the twelve wet and exhausted survivors over the rough ground to the lifeboat. As the twenty five men boarded the *Fair Maid of Perth*, the harbour tug undertook to tow the lifeboat back to harbour.

The tug pulled the lifeboat through the storm but before reaching the harbour the *Fair Maid of Perth* was swamped by three successive huge waves and overturned pitching all on board in to the icy sea. Some managed to grab hold of the tow rope whilst others held onto the upturned lifeboat. As the harbour tug proceeded slowly towards the pierhead the locals watched in horror at some men dangling from the tow rope. Many others held on grimly to the capsized lifeboat but this prevented it from self-righting. Now everyone was at the mercy of the cruel sea. Two lifeboat men Alex McEwan and William Grier sadly lost their lives that night along with two members of the shipwrecked crew. Coxswain Breckenridge was pulled from the water but died shortly afterwards from the effects of the cold and exhaustion.

Horse Island was the cause of yet another tragedy. At 11am on Monday 22nd November 1881 the 378-ton *Annetta*, a wooden hull barque, departed from Bowling. The barque was being towed by the Glasgow tug *Commodore* and was heading for the Port of Ardrossan to be loaded with coal. The *Annetta* crew members were Captain James Hoey, James Calligan, brothers Michael and Thomas Coogan, also John Smith, a twenty year old Ardrossan man who resided at the harbour houses and had been married for only four months. A friend of the crew, Daniel Robertson joined the vessel, "Just for a wee run to Ardrossan"

By 7pm as the vessels were rounding Horse Island the wind suddenly strengthened with great force and the tow cable snapped apart leaving the helpless *Annetta* to bear the full brunt of the storm. As the vessel drifted towards the island both anchors were thrown overboard and thankfully held the barque steady.

The *Commodore* left the scene and sailed to the harbour where the captain reported that the *Annetta* had dropped both anchors and was unlikely to run aground. The harbour tug *Terrier* had already set off to lend assistance but returned to its berth after meeting with the *Commodore* entering the harbour.

Mrs Boyd, wife of the owner, ordered the captain of *Commodore* to set back out immediately and bring the vessel in. The tug sailed through the mountainous seas in an attempt to reach the *Annetta*. After repeated unsuccessful efforts to sail close enough to get a tow rope aboard, the tug returned to the harbour where the captain reported that the anchors should hold fast, rendering the *Annetta* safe and that he would go out to bring her in at daylight.

Unfortunately the force of the winds became stronger and fears were expressed for the safety of the crew. As the evening wore on it became common knowledge to the locals that a ship was in distress. Anxiety became more intense when the large crowd gathered at the harbour became aware that John Smith from Ardrossan was on board. If the vessel dragged her anchors nothing could prevent her from foundering on the island rocks adding to the toll of ships already lost there.

At 11pm the lifeboat was launched but by now could make no headway through the appalling sea conditions. The heavy swell was being whipped up by the strong winds causing the waves to swamp the lifeboat. With heavy hearts the lifeboat crew battled their way back to the harbour. Nothing more could be done for the present and another rescue attempt would hopefully be made at first light.

With each passing hour the fury of the storm increased and the downpour of icy cold rain never relented. After long hours of riding out the violent storm the vessel dragged its anchors, was thrown against the rocks, then started to break up. By 4am Captain Hoey decided to abandon ship and try to get his crew on to Horse Island.

Michael Coogan, the vessel's mate volunteered to attempt to swim the narrow channel between the ship and the island. If successful he would secure a rope across the gap.

With a rope tied round his waist he plunged into the black, swirling water. Michael was a powerful swimmer and fought his way through the strong current. Four times he grabbed on to the shoreline rocks only to be washed back into the sea. At the fifth attempt he grasped hold of seaweed, growing on the rocks, which thankfully held his weight as he dragged himself ashore.

His fingers were numb and stiff with the cold as he struggled to untie the rope from his waist and secure it firmly to a rock.

Thomas Coogan was next to leave the vessel. As he was lashed to the rope he admitted that he could not swim but would put his trust in his brother to pull him safely across. As the terrified sailor was inched slowly towards his brother the rope sagged and poor Thomas was trapped between two rocks. In desperation to free himself Thomas untied the rope but lost his grip and instantly the current swept him out to sea.

John Smith from Ardrossan was next to be lashed to the rescue rope and hauled across. Unfortunately, due to the sagging of the rope he also became stuck in the rocks. John, stood little chance of survival with the heavy sea cascading over him. Michael tugged frantically on the rescue rope and at last managed to free his shipmate. He heaved hard on the rope, dragging John closer and closer to the island. During all of this time John could not keep his head above the water and struggled for air. When he was landed on the island Michael realised that his rescue efforts had been in vain as poor John Smith had drowned, so close to his home.

With two of his shipmates lost, Michael now realised that the slackness of the rope was causing the rescue operation to fail. He summoned all his strength and managed to tighten the rope.

James Calligan was next to be pulled across the gap. As he was dragged through the water his socks and shoes were lost to the battering waves. When James staggered ashore his bare feet were badly cut and bleeding but he had made it safely over.

On board the wreck Daniel Robertson, who had boarded the *Annetta* "Just for a wee run to Ardrossan" panicked and tried to swim to the island without the rope being tied around his waist. Daniel was wearing two heavy coats to keep out the cold and before he could be stopped he jumped overboard and was dragged under the waves, never to be seen again.

Only one man now remained on the wreck of the *Annetta*, Captain James Hoey. He surveyed what was left of his once proud ship and with a heavy heart dropped over the side to words of encouragement being shouted by his two remaining crewmen.

He gripped the rope tightly as it cut into his hands. When he felt his legs jar against the rocks and his feet touched solid ground he stumbled ashore.

The three survivors assessed the situation they were now in. Cold, wet and stranded on a small windswept island with no immediate hope of rescue. Their only chance of survival was to reach the tower on the southern tip. If they could muster the strength to fight their way across the rough ground with hidden deep icy pools, then at least they would have shelter from the harsh storm. The men supported each other as they staggered towards the tower, never taking their eyes from it, willing themselves to keep going.

On reaching the tower they were bent double by the strong blasts of wind that threatened to lift them off their feet. They then had to crawl on hands and knees up the nine steps to reach into the sanctuary.

Although now sheltered from the wind and rain the three survivors were still left in miserable conditions. The night was long in passing as they sat shivering in their wet clothes, listening as the storm still raged outside, praying for it to end. Michael was greatly distressed over the loss of his brother and

The fireplace in the tower

John Robertson

The nine steps into the tower

41

dreaded having to tell his parents. When dawn broke the high tide was covering most of the island, almost reaching up to the ninth step.

The morale of the three men huddled together in the tower was very low. They had witnessed three of their shipmates perish, they had no food and were suffering from the cold. Built within the tower was a fireplace and littered on the floor were pieces of wood, enough to kindle a fire and give them warmth. However they had no means of lighting one. As they watched out of the window towards the harbour, they knew in their own hearts that the weather would not allow any form of rescue attempt until the storm abated. Looking out in the opposite direction in the distance they could see a sailing ship heading their way. It appeared to them that the vessel was out of control as she was labouring under the heavy seas

Meantime some locals of Ardrossan who had gathered at the harbourside became excited. They were full of hope that the brig in the distance was involved in a rescue bid. However as the vessel swung to and fro it was obvious to all that the sailing ship was drifting helplessly, at the mercy of the storm. The locals watched hopefully towards the tower for any sign of life. They were witnessing two tragedies. Stranded on the rocks the wreck of the *Annetta* was still being pounded to pieces. Coming from the direction of the Isle of Arran the helpless sailing ship was now on a course that would bring her ashore between Ardrossan and Irvine. In the tower the shipwrecked mariners kept a watch with sinking hearts as their ship was breaking apart. They also watched anxiously from the opposite window as the other sailing ship pitched and tossed ever nearer. They were fearful for the safety of her crew.

Suddenly a huge wave crashed against the sailing ship causing her to roll dangerously to one side. Before she could right herself another almighty wave hit her and she sank beneath the sea. There was no sign of survivors.

Completely despondent the three shipwrecked mariners had witnessed the loss of two ships. Now they could do nothing but wait to be rescued. Early in the afternoon the storm began to settle slightly. The three men were now in a pitiful condition. Chilled and without food or water. Their wet clothes rubbed against the open sores on their bodies. The empty fireplace seemed to taunt them. One dry flint to light the fire could have lessened their suffering considerably. By 2pm still no effort had been made to rescue the men. The ever growing crowd on the harbourside were becoming increasingly vexed about the situation and anxious that the lifeboat should try to reach the stranded men. The harbour tug took the lifeboat in tow but returned after only a short time without reaching the island.

Four brave local men took the matter into their own hands by manning a small boat and setting off to attempt a rescue. The four James McGratton, James MacKay, James Scullion and William Miller rowed out of the harbour to the resounding cheers of the large crowd. By now it seemed as if the whole population of Ardrossan had turned out to watch. Regrettably the small boat was no match against the raging sea and two of the men were washed over the side and the oars lost. Fortunately they, along with the two others and the boat were all washed ashore. They even tried again but had to give up.

Around 4pm two small sailing boats each with a crew of four cast off to attempt a rescue. The crowds watched silently as the boats neared the island then loud cheers and shouts of joy broke out as the ships succeeded in reaching the men and taking them on board. The crowds were jubilant when at last the survivors were brought back safely to the harbour.

Later that day the sailing ship *Victoire* arrived at Ardrossan. The crew related the story of the brig that had been seen drifting helplessly before sinking. It was the *St Fillan* with no one on board. She had broken loose from her anchorage in Lamlash Bay and been carried away by the storm. The crew from the *St Fillan* had managed to scramble safely aboard the *Victoire* and came ashore at Ardrossan.

In 1894, another sea drama took place involving the 256-ton Norwegian registered brig, *Loven* of Christiania. The vessel was loaded with coal and carried a Scandinavian crew of eight. On the morning of Thursday 20 December, the vessel left Ardrossan Harbour with a full cargo of coal, bound for her registered port in Norway. Three miles south of Ailsa Craig, the weather took a turn for the worse and reached severe storm force. The *Loven* then made an attempt to reach the sheltered waters of Lamlash Bay, Isle of Arran.

As he approached the bay, the brig's captain, J Melsom, decided that due to the enormous waves driven by the ferocious winds and as he was unfamiliar with the entrance it would be safer to head back to Ardrossan Harbour. During the terrible voyage, severe difficulties were experienced with the south westerly gale blowing the vessel over, putting her in grave danger of capsizing.

Ardrossan town was also being battered by the hurricane winds. The local parish church had lost two of its turrets as they crashed to the ground. The main shopping street in the town was very severely damaged and many shop windows were blown out completely. Ardrossan Harbour offered no shelter now. As the heavy swelling waves surged into the harbour basin they collided with the retreating waves creating a furious boiling maelstrom which damaged many vessels and sank the schooner *Margaret Mitchell* at her moorings.

Out at sea, Captain Melsom battled hour after hour against the atrocious weather conditions. His brave crew climbed the masts to shorten the sails when the harbour lights came into view.

At 7 o'clock in the morning, as they made progress slowly towards the harbour the storm force wind changed direction. The sudden change caught the sails and drove the vessel onto the rocks close to Horse Island. Both anchors were dropped in a desperate attempt to save the ship but this proved fruitless as the vessel started to roll violently from side to side. The captain and four of his crew were caught in the grip of one of the giant waves, sweeping over the vessel, and washed overboard. The rest of the crew could only watch in horror. Almost immediately the *Loven* sank beneath the waves. The three remaining crewmen had to climb the main mast to keep themselves above water.

The volunteer lifeboat men prepared the lifeboat *Charles Skirrow* a small rowing boat with sails, for a rescue attempt. A desperate effort was made to reach the shipwreck. The three helpless seamen could be seen perched on the mast, which was still protruding above the water. The lifeboat could make no progress against the ferocious wind. The crew hauled on the oars until they were exhausted and finally had to admit defeat as the fierce wind drove them back into the harbour. By now the three men had been stranded on their perilous perch for six hours. Hope of survival was fading as the icy waves cascaded over them and the freezing wind threatened to rip them from the mast.

The captain of the *Glen Rosa*, a vessel berthed at the harbour, refused a request for the use of his ship's lifeboat to try to reach the three crewmen.

Mr MacGill of the Ardrossan Shipbuilding Yard offered one of his small rowing boats and asked for five volunteers. On hearing of this Archibald McMillan, William Plue, Neil Robertson and George Fabian, all from Saltcoats and James Boyd from Ardrossan offered their services immediately.

The people on the quayside shouted words of encouragement to the five brave volunteers as they set out on their mission of mercy. It was with fierce determination that each man heaved on the oars. They knew that if they failed to reach the sunken *Loven* the three sailors would be lost.

The small boat rode the waves and held its course against all the odds. Remarkably they managed to come close to the wreck. With great skill the rowing boat was positioned near enough for the three men to attempt to leap aboard. Each man had to time his jump carefully as the rescue vessel was being jostled violently by the waves. All three were successfully boarded and taken back in triumph to the cheers of the waiting crowd.

At the Court of Enquiry it was decided that the wind and weather was against the Ardrossan lifeboat crew when they made their brave rescue attempt but were forced to return to the harbour. The three Scandinavian survivors who had clung to the ship's mast for more than seven hours were O Olsen, Swerte Mahle and Victor E Nelson.

At a meeting in the town hall the five rescuers were each presented with the sum of sixteen pounds nine shillings. This was equivalent to three months wages, which indicated the high esteem held for the bravery of the volunteers who saved three lives in the most atrocious of conditions.

During March 1882 great sorrow was reported in the town on hearing of the death of one such much respected guardian of the local seas. Aleck Brodie had served for more than twenty years as head harbour pilot and was well liked locally. "Old Aleck" and his mates would spin many a yarn while ensconced by the cosy fire. He always kept an ever watchful eye for approaching lights on the horizon. He was said to make an impressive figure standing on the pierhead, always erect with a military disposition. No incoming or outgoing vessel was said ever to have received their orders in a more clear or commanding tone of voice at any other shipping port.

The Two Brigadiers
In the 1960s working tugs were very much in evidence escorting large oil tankers in and out through the narrow entrance of Ardrossan Harbour to and from the Shell Tanker Berth. It was a remarkable coincidence that two tugs bearing the same name should both become casualties on Horse Island, both victims of the same rocks.

The *Brigadier*, a 257 gross ton tug, owned by Steel and Bennie of Greenock departed from the Tail-o-the Bank very early on Sunday 20th February 1960 under the command of Captain William McKeague. Her destination was Ardrossan Harbour where she would assist the Ardrossan tug *Seaway* in towing the Norwegian tanker *Mosborg* out of the tanker berth. The *Mosborg* had been discharging her cargo of crude oil for the Shell Refining and Marketing Company. On clearing the harbour the tanker was due to sail that day to the Persian Gulf.

At anchor, a quarter of a mile out to sea was another Norwegian tanker, the *Norfoss* with a cargo of oil fuel. The *Norfoss* was waiting to be towed into the tanker berth when the *Mosborg* departed.

For the previous four days Ardrossan and the surrounding area had been suffering from bad snowstorms which had caused havoc including the derailment of three light engines during shunting operations. A heavy snowplough was unable to clear the snow off the main roads due to abandoned cars and at nearby Hunterston Nuclear Power Station construction work had to be stopped.

The *Brigadier* – come to grief on Horse Island

As the *Brigadier* approached the harbour the atrocious weather was waiting with a vengeance. A blinding snow storm swept along the coast creating a complete white-out. At 5.45am there was a huge crunch as the tug ran aground on the submerged shelves at the southern tip of Horse Island. Once again the island had trapped and held another victim. As the *Brigadier* shuddered to a halt one of the crew was almost thrown overboard. Another was tossed from his bunk bed and landed unceremoniously on the deck.

The bottom of the vessel was badly holed and water quickly flooded into the engine room. The engineers had to wade through the deepening water to escape up the ladder to the open deck.

From the port control tower the harbour pilot, Captain Neil MacDonald saw the tug's lights go out and

The *Bally Halbert* aground on 9 January 1958

James Macgregor

knew she had struck the rocks. He quickly ordered his two boatmen John Thomson and Eddie O'Boyle to accompany him in taking the pilot boat out to render immediate assistance. As they cast off the mooring ropes the sky was suddenly lit up by the distress rockets sent up from the marooned tug.

In very choppy sea conditions Captain MacDonald successfully manoeuvred the pilot boat alongside the *Brigadier* which enabled the eight stranded crewmen to jump on board. The captain of the tug decided to remain with his vessel to assess the damage.

As the *Brigadier* seemed to be held firmly on the rocks the pilot boat set off for the harbour leaving the Ardrossan tug *Seaway* to stand by the stranded tug. The pilot boat returned to Horse Island and once more drew alongside the tug. Having ascertained the damage to his vessel Captain McKeague jumped on board the pilot boat and was taken to the harbour.

The *Brigadier* was so badly damaged the insurance company wrote the vessel off as a complete wreck. Metal Industries Ltd Faslane, Gareloch were awarded the contract to break up the tug for salvage. Nine months later the remains of the *Brigadier* were still sitting abandoned on the rocks. It was being broken up bit by bit by a Greenock man who was only able to do the job when the weather permitted.

A new tug was named *Brigadier* and she carried out her duties without mishap until Friday 24th February 1967. Then by a quirk of fate the vessel also became stuck fast on the Horse Island shelves at almost the same spot. The tug had just towed out a tanker and cleared the harbour safely, when on releasing the tow rope a wire became entangled in the tug's propeller and stopped the engine.

Without any power the tug drifted helplessly towards Horse Island. The crew braced themselves as the tug crunched onto the rocks. As the *Brigadier* was stuck fast the crew were taken off for their own safety. The following day the crew were taken out in an attempt to refloat the vessel. Due to stormy sea conditions they had to be taken back off again.

The next day the crew and three employees of the Ardrossan Dockyard Company, J Whylie, H Townsley and

Angus McLaughlan were taken out to the stranded vessel. After Angus McLaughlan burned the wire free of the propeller the tug was refloated under her own power. As the *Brigadier* had suffered damage to her steering, it was arranged that the vessel would go into the dry dock at Ardrossan for repairs.

The navigation marker fixed onto a rock, known as The Perch was the scene of a sea drama with a fateful outcome in 1949

The picture below shows just how close to Horse Island the marker is

A Christmas Tragedy

Robert Hunter, aged 43, was employed by the Ardrossan Harbour Company as a foreman bricklayer. Although a non swimmer he was also the company diver. He lived in one of the company's new houses at 5 Alfred's Square, Ardrossan, with his wife Mary and daughter Nancy.

Robert had enjoyed a successful professional football career having played with Clyde at Shawfield, Glasgow and

also with Portadown. He had been secretary to the local Saltcoats Victoria Club for a number of years. His two brothers Alex and Adam were also well-known football players. On the morning of Wednesday 28th December 1949, Robert set off for work in high spirits. Mary was busily preparing for the evening ahead as they were to have a night out together attending a dance in Stevenston. Young Nancy was going to stay overnight with friends.

A few days previously a dreadful storm had swept the area causing much damage. A navigation marker fixed onto a rock, known as The Perch, had snapped and tumbled into the sea. The twenty feet (6 metres) high unlit wrought iron marker with a large ornamental globe on top, warned of the dangerous submerged shelves of Horse Island.

Harbour Master Captain William Paterson Brock had been waiting for favourable weather conditions to sanction the repairs necessary on the rock before a new marker could be erected. That morning the weather was calm although extremely cold. The harbour master instructed Robert to take James Frew, his 21 year-old apprentice, out to repair the foundation.

At 10am the two men were ferried out in a small motor launch and landed on the rock with their tools. It was agreed that the motor launch would return for them at 11.30am as the job should take no more than one and a half hours to complete.

The men were engrossed in their task of cutting away the damaged foundation and didn't at first notice the wind rising and whipping up the waves. The harbour master became anxious about the sudden deterioration in the weather and sent out the small boat at 11.10am to retrieve the two workmen.

The waves began breaking over the rock making the two men increasingly anxious to get off. Feeling nervous they watched as the boat returned for them. It was obviously having great difficulty in coping with the turbulent sea. Captain Reginald Knox, the harbour pilot had been alerted and quickly made his way to the pilot boat where he was joined by the crew. They headed out to The Perch where the high wind was now lashing the waves over the two distressed men stranded on the rock.

The crew of the pilot boat were also struggling in their rescue attempt as their vessel was being buffeted about by the high waves. On realising it was impossible to get alongside the rock the crew sailed as close as they dared and frantically threw lifebelts. This was of no help as the current carried the lifebelts away from the men.

As the small motor launch was being tossed high by the waves and was in imminent danger of capsizing, the pilot boat proceeded to escort the smaller vessel back to the harbour before making another attempt to rescue the men.

The harbour master was monitoring the critical situation his two workmen were now in. As he stood in the control tower watching through binoculars, the cold waves surged ever higher over the men abandoned on the rock at the mercy of the wild sea. It was regrettable that the Ardrossan lifeboat was no longer at hand to render assistance in this dreadful situation. In 1930 the lifeboat station had been transferred to Troon.

Robert and James were alarmed to see the two rescue vessels turn away from them and retreat back to the harbour. It now seemed their only chance of survival was to get themselves on to Horse Island which was only about eighteen feet (5.4 metres) distance away with two protruding rocks in between. Robert shouted to his apprentice that their only hope was to enter the water and make for the nearest rock then the next rock. From there they could reach the safety of Horse Island and seek sanctuary in the tower.

Both men quickly took off their boots, overcoats and jackets. Robert, bravely entered the freezing water first, followed by his apprentice. The fierce current caught both men and swept them past the first rock. They now had to make a desperate effort to catch a hold on the next rock. Robert was carried away in the grip of the savage sea. James was more fortunate in being close enough to grab onto the second rock and managed to hold on grimly before pulling himself on top of it. As the waves lashed over him he looked frantically for Robert and was distraught when he saw him being swept helplessly past the island and out to the open sea.

James lay on the rock to regain his breath before he plunged once more into the cold water and managed to struggle ashore on Horse Island. When the pilot boat speedily returned to The Perch, to the crew's utter consternation there was now no one on the rock. A figure was sighted on Horse Island and the pilot guided his boat to the sheltered side of the island to reach the sole survivor. The apprentice James was helped on board and taken down to the warm engine room. On arrival at the harbour he was taken by ambulance to his home at 36 Townhead, Stevenston, only two doors away from where Robert's parents lived. Unfortunately help had come too late for Robert. A search was carried out until 3.15pm but no sign of the missing man was found.

The following day a search party sailed round Horse Island in an endeavour to recover the body. On board the vessel was Police Constable Joseph Armour, Assistant Harbour Master Lindsay Trail and George Hall, a harbour boatman. A careful and diligent search was made of the island and the surrounding rocks but sadly Robert's body was never recovered.

Lifeboats
Ardrossan has been very thankful for the presence of the lifeboats and their brave volunteer crews. Since 1820 when the town's short range lifeboat came into service there have been four RNLI lifeboats.
The FAIR MAID OF PERTH served for 23 years from 1870 until 1893. This was followed by the CHARLES SKIRROW which was replaced in 1899 by the JAMES STEVENS No 8.
The JAMES AND JOHN YOUNG provided service from 1913 until 1930 when the RNLI closed the station and moved their services to Troon. During their 60 years sterling service the crew of the four lifeboats saved a total of 132 lives. The people of Ardrossan were sorry to lose the lifeboat station from their harbour.

Horse Island from Ardrossan's North
Shore – scene of many a shipping
accident

MEMORIES OF HORSE ISLAND

Horse Island is looked on by the town of Ardrossan and so quite naturally it figures to some extent in the minds of the populace. An island which appears to be just within reach but yet just untouchable holds a strange fascination for young and old alike. On the following pages some residents relate their thoughts about Horse Island and the efforts to reach this haunting landfall.

JOHN KELLY

During the 1920s a few local men saved up some of their hard-earned money to buy their own small boats. The boats were put to good use as all summer they enabled the men to lay creels to catch lobsters and other sea food from the rich beds around Horse Island. This was a good way to help feed the large families and also to supplement the weekly income.

Hugh Kelly, remembered here by his son John, was a skilled boatman who worked with Ardrossan Harbour Company for 52 years

During this period there were many houses situated within the harbour area. In one of the houses beside the dock gates lived the Kelly family – Hugh Kelly along with his wife Rose-Ann and their children. Next door to their house was a large warehouse which caught fire causing them to be evacuated and rehoused at 7 Harbour Buildings.

More children were born to the happy parents and when the number reached eleven, two girls and nine boys, the family were allocated a larger house back beside the dock gates. Hugh was employed as a crane-man by the harbour company for fifty two years. During the 1939/1945 war he had, at one time, six boys all serving their country. Two in the army, two in the Royal Navy and two in the Merchant Navy.

One of the sons, John, still resides near the harbour with his wife, Maureen, in a comfortable new house with a splendid view of the Firth of Clyde. He spends many a happy hour looking out of his window to Horse Island remembering his happy childhood. John brings back to mind how during the long school holidays one or two of the boys would be allowed to accompany their father to attend to his creels in the family boat, which was an eighteen feet (5.5 metres) converted lifeboat.

Hugh was a skilled boatman and taught his sons to respect the sea. When it became known that a trip was pending the boys would rush to get their boots on then race to the boat. The first ones to jump aboard secured a place for themselves and were taken on the trip.

When they reached the age of ten years the boys had gained enough knowledge and were trusted to be in charge of the boat by themselves. This was what they looked forward to most of all.

On these sunny, carefree days the boys would venture out to the island and spend the day investigating every nook and cranny. Although they didn't take a picnic with them the boys never went hungry. Their smoky old billy can was always taken. The rocks on the shore line were thickly covered with bunches of whelks which were easily picked off to fill the billy can. They soon had a fire started from driftwood and in next to no time the whelks were boiled up to provide a tasty meal for the hungry Kelly brothers. The happy youngsters were not alone out on the island. During the summer months there was always a herd of cattle to be found grazing on the lush grass. The boys had been well taught by their father on the art of seamanship and during their many excursions they never came to any harm.

The solitude of the island changed dramatically in the 1930s when motor boats from Saltcoats Harbour started making trips out to Horse Island. This venture proved to be very popular with the fare paying passengers who were left to wander for about one hour before returning back to Saltcoats.

MAY CONVERY

During the long summer school holidays children were left to amuse themselves. They had no fancy toys or bikes and television was unheard of in those bygone times. There was certainly no money to spare for outings. Life was happy and carefree and families stayed close to home.

One special day in 1923 is fixed in May's memory. Her next door neighbour, in Bradshaw Street Saltcoats, Mr Blair, was planning to take his daughter Grace on a picnic over to Horse Island and he had invited May to join them. The best friends eagerly awaited to be taken on this great adventure and made plans for their forthcoming visit to the island.

When the great day finally arrived the two little eight year old girls could hardly contain their excitement. Jam sandwiches had been carefully prepared and packed into a basket along with a special treat, a bottle of home made lemonade.

The adventure began at Saltcoats Railway Station. The girls all dressed up for the occasion watched as the big noisy train ground to a halt amid great billows of hissing steam. They clambered aboard escorted by Mr Blair. They had hardly been seated when within minutes the train had arrived at their destination, "Caley" Station Ardrossan. (The station was opened on 4th September 1888 as Ardrossan North but all the locals referred to it as "The Caley" as it was owned by the Caledonian Railway Company.)

May and her friend hurried along the beach, trying to keep up with Grace's dad as he strode quickly along to hire a rowing boat to take them out to Horse Island. When all three were safely settled on board, the boat set off (there were no lifebelts in those days). The sea was a bit choppy and with the sheer excitement of it all May was soon sick.

But once reaching the island May's sickness was completely forgotten. As they scrambled ashore the boatman made a note in his little book at what time he was to return for them. He then sailed back to the harbour leaving them to their own devices.

They spent a pleasant few hours walking all over the island. It was so beautiful carpeted in wild flowers and the birds wheeling and calling overhead.

The girls sat on the grass, in the warm sunshine, to eat their picnic. As they gazed over to the mainland Grace's dad pointed out the familiar landmarks. Everything looked so different when viewed from "across the sea".

All too soon the little boat came into view coming back to take them away from this enchanting island. The memory of that day remains clear to May seventy six years later.

JOHN ROBERTSON

John Robertson was well known in the cyclist's world. His excellent hand-built bicycles were much sought after. He was and still is a keen cyclist and used to take part in road races all over Britain, winning over eighty cups. He won the 125-mile Andalucia race in Spain and was second past the winning post in the World Champion Race in Germany.

All week long John looked forward to the weekend. Sunday was the day that could be spent on long cycling trips. With a friend he would leave Glasgow to cycle down round the Ayrshire coast and back to Glasgow.

One hot afternoon whilst stopping for a break at Ardrossan's North Shore the boys noticed the little island, situated not too far out from the beach, and wondered about it. John's interest in Horse Island was kindled that day fifty years ago when he saw it for the first time. Instead of just sitting admiring the view the pair of them decided to swim out to have a closer look.

As they swam out in stages, from rock to rock, the birds were wheeling and dipping overhead and lots of seals were lazily basking on the rocks.

On reaching the island they watched a group of porpoises making their way past on the seaward side, gracefully swimming and ducking in unison through the waves. What could be more idyllic than this, thought John as they made their way back.

The years passed but John never forgot his visit and always wanted to return. He didn't go again until 1996, by which time he lived within sight of the island. His wife Dorothy agreed to accompany him as long as he did not intend to swim out this time.

After receiving permission from the RSPB to land there and take photographs he sailed out in his dinghy with Dorothy and Rusty, their well-behaved little pet dog. They spent a lovely afternoon taking photographs and walking round the island.

Whilst sitting beside the tower enjoying a picnic they noticed a plaque, above the doorway, too high up to read. Dot was told that they would have to come back again with ladders to enable him to read the inscription.

On their next trip, determined as ever, John tried to tow ladders out but they kept sinking. John's next ingenious idea was to balance the ladders across the dinghy. Dot and Rusty were instructed not to move as they proceeded slowly over to the landing place on the island. All went well and the ladders were carried to the tower. As Dorothy held them firmly in place John climbed up to read the words. After 185 years the inscription was so badly eroded that he had to trace the words with chalk to make them out.

The words engraved in 1811 were,

SITED BY HUGH,
12th EARL OF EGLINTON.
SUGGESTED BY JOHN ROSS.

When it was time to go, much to Dorothy's relief the ladders were left out on the island.

CORALIE CAMPBELL

a day out to Horse Island in the 1950s for Coralie Campbell and family

Coralie Campbell, daughter of the late Captain Ian Duart Campbell, was an only child. She remembers how she would eagerly await her father's return home from faraway places. How thrilled she was to listen as he spoke of all the exciting destinations he had visited, such as Canada, South Africa and the West Indies. Coralie grew up in Ardrossan and there was one island that always seemed to beckon her. Horse Island was within sight of her home and she longed to visit it. Coralie relates this delightful tale.

"During school holidays in the early fifties I would spend endless summer days, along with my dear friend Elspeth and cousins Pat and Carl, climbing and playing on the nearby Long Craigs rocks. Horse Island was tantalizingly close. One morning at low tide, thinking we could walk onto it, we confidently set out for the farthest point. Alas the isle which had seemed so near was separated from us by a deep stretch of water.

Our plan was thwarted but in our imaginary world, fired by stories such as *Swallows and Amazons* and the Famous Five, there must be a solution! Having no boat we planned to build ourselves a raft.

Our desire to spend days cooped up in a garden shed aroused suspicion just as the table top raft was almost completed. My father, a world travelled master mariner, home on leave, lost no time in questioning our knowledge of the rocks, tides and currents. By the time he'd finished our hearts were at rock bottom, for the visit to our magic island, almost within our grasp, now necessitated the most treacherous voyage on the seven seas. We didn't ask how he as a young lad had sailed with friends on any old makeshift raft from the harbour and lived to tell the tale.

Later, plan three was put into action, my father knew all the dangers so why didn't he take us? To our delight he agreed.

Sadly for us, leave for this Master Mariner didn't coincide with school holidays till three of us were well into our teens but the promise was kept and the wait did not lessen our rapture when it was announced that Hughie Kelly at the harbour had agreed to take us in his motor launch. The plans of four years before were put into action. The list of food was resurrected with little thought given to my mother's work providing our agreed choice of ham and egg pies, a lemon meringue pie and home-made lemonade!

The old tent and travel arrangements were checked. The little map of the island was carefully placed in an envelope, the map to be completed on our return with places of interest and discoveries marked.

The long awaited day, 17th August 1957, dawned bright and clear. How could it have been otherwise! Carl, one of the original plotters, had not yet arrived but his little sister Lynn took his place. Another cousin Paddy had newly arrived from Burma on *MV Derbyshire* and was full of enthusiasm for another voyage but she insisted that as she was now in Scotland, Uncle Ian, (my father), must go and change into his kilt.

Soon we were leaving the harbour behind, trailing our hands in the cool water, as the little boat chugged over the short stretch of sea to the fulfilment of childhood dreams.

My first impression of the island was a sea of mayweed in the sunlit grass and all around the shimmering blue under a never ending sky. Our excitement knew no bounds and having landed near the tower, we made a beeline for it. There my father carved our initials, for the benefit of posterity. Paddy requested that her name be written in full. Whether or not that happened we cannot now recall but certainly my father joked about future visitors thinking an Irishman had stopped en route to Scotland or perhaps hopped across from "Paddy's Milestone"! (Ayrshire's name for the island of Ailsa Craig in the Firth of Clyde)

Our recollection of the story of some family who had lived for a month there in the summer, is vague. Were they gathering mussels or such like? Tales were told too of cattle being taken out from Montfode Farm and we liked the story of horses swimming ashore, a much more romantic reason for the name than the derivation from Philip de Horsse.

Having made our claim on the island and heard some of the stories we set off across shallow water to the sandy bay we'd gazed at with interest four years previously, from the Long Craigs Rocks.

Our little green tent was pitched before we explored for treasure from wrecks. Broken pieces of blue patterned tiles intrigued us. We didn't bring any back but we did find a wooden spade which was marked later with the date when brought home as a memento. Smoothed by the sea it was stroked by us as we imagined its journey, tempest-tossed from some distant shore.

We all changed into our bathing suits in the tent except for little Lynn who ran out half clad shouting, "Come on out girls there's nobody here." We bathed there and still recall the view of sea creatures, shells and stones on the sandy floor, so pellucid was the deep water. We signalled to landlubbers with towels. We ate our lunch and praised the cook. We explored. Hughie Kelly appeared from nowhere and the two men had a stroll to the seaward side of the island to allow us time on our own.

Elspeth, Lynn and I took the southern end whilst Pat and Paddy made for the centre. Great was the excitement when they came racing over to tell us they'd seen a rabbit. The rest of the visit was spent hunting for the poor beast which had of course wisely gone to ground.

Too soon the captain and Hughie Kelly had finished their smoke and called for us to make ready. Calling "Ship ahoy" to each other we raced to pack up then made our slow trail to the landing place at the north. It was explained this was to accord with the tide. (Making us more aware of our past childhood folly and of superior knowledge).

We returned to relate the excitement of the days adventure to mother and auntie. Though well into our teens, apart from Lynn, when our dreams became reality, that day on "our" desert isle was indeed magic."

IAN FRASER AND GORDON FRASER

Two brothers from Stevenston, Ian and Gordon Fraser have had a lifelong interest in the habits of wild birds. When they were young boys they used to escape into the countryside every Sunday when relations came to visit. It was much more interesting to be out and about finding bird's nests and observing the customs of the different species than sitting at home.

Horse Island was where they wished to visit most as it was teeming with bird life. In 1944 their Uncle Andy took the boys out to the island for the first time. During this era many people would go out to collect the gulls' eggs which were plentiful and the old fish boxes that had been washed up on the island were used to carry the eggs back home. Some of the eggs were handed into the local hospital and gratefully received as during the war years hen's eggs were hard to come by.

This trip fired the brothers' enthusiasm to further investigate all the varying bird life on the island. Saltcoats boatman, Jimmy Reid took them out on numerous other occasions and as Ian and Gordon's interest grew they began counting and photographing the different birds. Ian was particularly fascinated as he watched the large Skuas chasing after the little Terns. The Tern would duck and dive in an attempt to shake off its determined pursuer. The larger bird could anticipate every move as the Tern whirled around while keeping a tight grip on its catch of little fish in its beak. The tiny Tern could only end the chase by letting go of its catch. The Skua would then swoop and snatch the fish in mid air.

The first time they ventured out by themselves from Saltcoats Harbour it was a fine sunny day. The small rowing boat skimmed over the calm sea and they reached the island in next to no time. When it was time to return however the weather had changed. A blustery wind had risen making the sea very choppy.

On the return journey to Saltcoats the boys found it hard going holding the boat on course as it was being tossed about by the heavy waves. Jimmy Reid, the boatman noticed the change in the sea conditions and was concerned about the brothers in their small rowing boat. He headed out in his motor launch to tow them back. When he reached them Ian and Gordon refused the offer of a tow as their pride would have been dented. They gallantly battled on through the waves pulling hard on the oars. They were never so glad to reach Saltcoats Harbour and wished they had accepted the offer of a tow.

With each visit to the island the brothers interest increased. They searched all over trying to find a source of fresh water, but never did find the existence of a spring.

Another time they climbed the vertical ladders which were fixed to the inside of the tower. On reaching the small upper floor they discovered this was where the harbour company housed the battery which powered the red light sited on top of the tower. Much to their amusement perched on top of the light was a crow's nest. The two crows were enjoying the central heating being provided from the warning light.

The brothers were very keen to compile a census and collate a photographic record of all the existing birds. This undertaking could only be possible if they stayed on Horse Island for a week or two. Plans were soon under way for this project. The friendly boatman agreed to take them out with all the necessary equipment such as camping gear, provisions and the all important milk churn filled with fresh water. Every few days a fresh churn of water was ferried out to them.

The venture began on a fine sunny Saturday morning with Jimmy Reid helping to load the boys gear on to his boat before heading out to the island. The skilled boatman pulled alongside a large flat rock near the tower and told the boys to jump. The boat was rising and falling in the swell. As they were trying to gauge when best to jump Jimmy got anxious about the bottom of his boat being damaged by 'the rocks. He shouted, "Jump now or I will kick you off." After leaping ashore all their gear swiftly followed as it was tossed over to them from the boat.

The next morning dawned cold and wet. A heavy downpour continued all day, the rain battering down on the little tent. Undaunted Ian and Gordon carried on with their self-appointed task. Monday and Tuesday the rain never ceased but undeterred they still got on with what they wanted to do. The ground became water logged and the little tent all but sailed away.

By Wednesday they decided to move into the tower to try to gain some shelter from the elements. The small tent was pitched in the wide doorway. Gordon recalls it was like living in a fridge. The supply of sausages and bacon stayed fresh in the freezing cold. They had brought with them lengths of hessian and broom handles to construct a hide. Hessian is ideal for bird watching as it allows the birds to be viewed through the material whilst concealing the watcher. They assembled the hide in the little niche between the tower steps and wall. This proved to be an effective shelter. At dusk the brothers awaited the regular visit of a Peregrine Falcon. The Tern colony would be in uproar at the approach of the Falcon from its eyrie on the nearby island of Little Cumbrae.

The brothers were too involved and dedicated to their project to let the adverse weather hinder them. One thing puzzled them – how did the rabbits survive the winter when the waves swept over their burrows?

Gordon could foresee the Tern would soon have to struggle for their existence against the Herring Gulls. He was instrumental in bringing the island under the control of the RSPB. Once the island was made a bird sanctuary Gordon was appointed warden along with Robert Arnott who had his own boat. Robert provided the means of transport for Gordon to do his bird counts. To fire the interest of the local schoolchildren Gordon would accompany groups of ten with their teacher on information walking tours around the island. Through the years the brothers have amassed an unequalled collection of photographs and slides of the island's wildlife. They have always been in demand for talks and slide presentations and today still give much of their time freely.

Gordon could foresee the Tern would soon have to struggle for their existence against the Herring Gulls

Cllr DAVID GALLAGHER

Well-known local councillor David Gallagher recalls his memories of Horse Island. As a youth he had been very keen on swimming and was often to be found, with his friends, at the open air swimming pool in Saltcoats. The midnight swimming sessions were then a particular favourite. When he was a schoolboy swimming lessons had been compulsory. Some of the pupils tried to avoid entering the cold water and would invent all sorts of excuses. David and his school mates looked forward to the visits to the pool and never seemed to feel the cold.

As the pupils became strong swimmers they were encouraged to tackle a mile-long swim in the sea. The swim commenced at the bathing pool in Saltcoats and finished at the rocky area of Ardrossan, known locally as "The Inches." Every one who succeeded in their attempt was rewarded with a certificate. After leaving school David and his three teenage friends continued to swim in the sea on a regular basis and to further test their swimming capabilities they decided to swim out to Horse Island. On reaching their goal the boys rested for a short time before swimming back to the North Shore, Ardrossan. The island held no interest for them only the swim out to it. They were to do this without mishap on numerous other occasions.

After a number of years the boys acquired a small punt with a little outboard engine. Now they could sail over to the island from Saltcoats Harbour. The use of the little boat brought a new perspective to their outings. Although they could now spend more time out there they were never tempted to wander over the island as it was by now a bird sanctuary. Saltcoats seemed a million miles away as they lay on the grass, without a care in the world.

David remembers how they would each bring a can of beer to drink while lying in the sunshine. Although the beer would be a little bit warm it always seemed to quench the thirst better, when out there on Horse Island.

JAMES SOMERS MACGREGOR

James has enjoyed a lifelong love of ships and the sea. He very much enjoyed his years associated with Ardrossan Harbour, commencing employment as a boatman's boy with the self-employed harbour pilots in 1946. Three years later he joined the harbour company as a boatman. James finished his happy working years in the port control tower. During thirty years of his service he was also a member of the auxiliary coastguard.

One incident that happened in 1946 still makes James smile. Captain Paddy Barclay was returning to the harbour in the pilot boat *Ardrossan* when the engine failed. The boat was stranded between Horse Island and the breakwater. James set off with Bobby Arnott in his boat to assist. When they drew alongside, Bobby held his boat steady as James leapt aboard the pilot boat. On reaching the cabin and pulling open the door thick smoke came pouring out. Sitting in the midst of the smoke-filled cabin was Captain Barclay, wearing an old cork life jacket, puffing away on his pipe creating great billows of smoke. A tow rope was secured and the pilot boat was taken safely back to the harbour.

During the summer of 1950 two local lads Archie McKenzie and

Donald Murchie sailed out to the island to collect eggs. During their visit the weather took a change for the worse and they couldn't get back because of the rough sea. The boys were observed through binoculars and as they were seen to be in no danger it was decided to leave them overnight to shelter in the tower. Archie McKenzie's father walked to the North Shore and stood firing his gun as a signal to the boys that he was aware of the situation. The next morning the weather had settled and the police went out with the rescue launch to reprimand the two boys for the trouble and worry they had caused.

Many other incidents were attended to through the years but during the summer of 1976 one family set off from the North Shore to picnic on the island. Dad, mum and two children settled into their 16 feet (4.8 metres) clinker built dinghy. They sat beside the provisions and a supply of beer anticipating a good day out. The small boat even had a fitted carpet.

Unfortunately the Arran ferry was approaching as the family were making their way out past the breakwater. Captain Alex Ferrier sounded the ship's horn as a warning and the man pulled furiously on the oars to get out of the way of the ferry.

Ardrossan Harbour Master Captain Tom Scott ordered James to go out in the rope-running boat and take the dinghy in tow into the harbour as they were a danger to themselves.

The family had reached Horse Island and were about to make a landing when James fixed a rope to their boat. They were towed to the harbour, protesting loudly all the way, to face the wrath of Captain Scott as they had almost caused a serious incident.

On inspection the dinghy was found to be in such a dangerous state Captain Scott ordered it to be lifted out of the water by crane and taken to the burning station for disposal.

The island will always attract a small number of adventurous local youngsters. All manner of transport has been devised to achieve the short sea journey. Some methods are ingenious whilst others are downright dangerous. Here follows a typical example of the exploits of some local youths during the 1970s.

JOCK KEAN

Jock was brought up in Ardrossan, one of five children of Robert (Bob) and Marion (Minnie) Kean. During the early fifties the local boys spent summer days down at the beach swimming in the sea. Jock with his pals Neil McCallum and Joseph (Jose) Farrel were very adventurous and decided to build a raft to carry them over to the island.

Beside the bus garage in Princess Street was the dumping ground for old bus tyres and inner tubes. When the garage was closed the boys would have a good rummage around looking for inner tubes that were not too badly punctured. Their selection of tubes was duly carried home for repair. Once all the holes had been patched using their bicycle repair kit, the task of blowing up the large rubber rings began. When three tubes stayed inflated they were tied together to make a raft. Planks of wood made excellent paddles.

The first sunny day when the sea was calm, they carried the raft out as far as possible on the North Shore. The three then paddled out to the nearest rock. After a rest they re-entered the water and paddled towards the next rock. It was great fun except when the one of the bus tyre inner tubes would deflate and the other two boys had to tow the deflated tube with their friend clinging on, out to the island.

They liked to walk over to the other side of Horse Island to see the seals basking lazily on the rocks. Keeping a watchful eye for the tide to turn, the boys were always ready to push the raft into the water and allow the tide to carry them back to the mainland. Later when Neil McCallum got a small dinghy the three boys would row over to the island during the breeding season to collect seagulls' eggs. There were always plenty of fish boxes washed up among the rocks. The boys always picked out the best one, then carried it all round the island to be filled with the gulls' eggs. While they were collecting the eggs the agitated gulls would dive-bomb them furiously. To prevent injury Jock and his two pals would remove their pullovers and wave them above their heads to frighten off the gulls. When they had collected sufficient eggs the dinghy was lined with grass and the eggs gently placed on board. The eggs were always delivered to Paddy McGill who fed them to his racing greyhounds.

The biggest problem ever encountered was when the weather changed unexpectedly for the return voyage and the sea would become choppy. Their confidence and swimming capabilities never let them down and they always reached the North Shore safely, completely unaware they had been in any danger. Now that Jock and his wife Meg have four children and seven grandchildren, he looks back with great consternation on the trips he made out to Horse Island as a boy.

IAN DOUGLAS

As a lad in 1976 Ian worked as a milk boy to earn money to buy a wet suit for diving. With his pals he would go diving in and around the harbour. On one occasion Ian and three of his friends set off for the island with a small dinghy. They had no oars so therefore they had to improvise. Two boys sat in the dinghy and two swam behind wearing flippers while pushing the dinghy in front of them.

All went well until the return journey when it was getting dark. As they neared the inner harbour marker buoy they suddenly noticed the approaching Arran ferry. Undeterred they held on grimly to the buoy as the wash from the ferry surged over them.

Little did they know they were being observed by Nelson Cook, who was on duty in the control tower. Nelson telephoned Ian's parents from the control tower to advise them what had happened and that they were now safely ashore. Ian had to hide the boat as his mother threatened to put an axe through it. Ian keeps a careful watch on his three young sons as they are all good swimmers and also have their dad's sense of adventure.

DAVID FITZPATRICK

David and two other men are employed on a rota system for duty as Port Controller with one always in attendance. David spends his working day high up in the port control tower at Ardrossan Harbour scanning the sea. He is responsible for the safe entry and exit of all vessels large and small.

A good clear view of the whole of Horse Island is seen from the tower and anyone landing on the island is immediately observed. If anyone should go on to the island the duty control tower staff at once notify the RSPB at Lochwinnoch, resulting in the police waiting at the harbourside for the return of the unauthorized island visitors.

On one occasion some boys built a line of fires, from the driftwood around the island. The police were called out to deal with the culprits as anything that disturbs the birds is not tolerated.

Local whelk collectors gather a good harvest from the rocks on the westward side. They respect the bird sanctuary and never set foot on the island.

On summer evenings organised groups depart from the beach at South Crescent in canoes and paddle all round Horse Island before returning at a steady pace back to the beach. They never disturb the birds or attempt to land.

Sometimes small craft unfamiliar with the area sail in the dangerous stretch of water between the mainland and the island. Many a propeller shaft has been damaged by the rocks.

Summer brings the usual mishaps with boys floating on inner tubes or airbeds out from the beach. The tide usually carries them out to the island.

Port controller David and his two colleagues George Campbell and Kenny Marriott have averted many a serious incident by promptly alerting Troon Lifeboat to the situation.

IMPRESSIONS

As a visit to Horse Island was essential we sought permission from the RSPB. On explaining the purpose they were very supportive and explained that we would have to wait until late summer when the breeding season would be over. Local man John Robertson (JR) had offered to ferry us out when the weather was favourable. As our house overlooks the island we watched all summer long its changing moods, while eagerly anticipating our trip.

Sunday 30th August 1998 dawned a brilliant summer's day with not a cloud in the clear blue sky. The island looked serene and peaceful surrounded by the shimmering sea. We had just a short distance to travel down to the beach at North Crescent, Ardrossan for the grand launching of JR's rubber dinghy.

After a short briefing the three of us were soon aboard and heading out towards the harbour breakwater. We could see at close hand the terrible damage the previous winter's storms had caused. The wall had been breached and was badly in need of repair. It was astounding to realise that the power of the waves could cause such damage.

JR pointed out to us how to navigate a safe course avoiding the many rocks and reefs. It is an extremely hazardous journey out to the one safe landing place on Horse Island and only an experienced seaman with good local knowledge would undertake it. JR has sailed these waters for many years and knows the area from every angle. As a qualified pilot he has flown over the island on many occasions.

As we headed over across the sparkling calm water the

island seemed to be further away than it appears from the shore. On approaching nearer the jagged teeth of the shoreline rocks became highlighted against the skyline, a dire threat to any vessel sailing within their reach and the need for the beacon tower became very apparent.

The tall tower is seen from a great distance as a warning to shipping to steer well clear of the perilous underwater shelves that surround the island. The wooden vessels of the early nineteenth century couldn't have stood much of a chance after being swept onto these razor sharp rocks. It was too awful to think of the poor sailors trying to scramble to safety while the rough sea pounded over them.

As we sailed round the southern tip of the island a surprisingly pleasant scene greeted us. Many seals were lying stretched out on the rocks sunbathing. As the waves gently lapped around them they dozed in the sunshine. A huge bull seal swam in our direction and lifted his large head to look our way. He watched us for a few moments then lost interest and swam away. We were glad since he was bigger than our dinghy and could easily have flipped it over. A few boats were plying to and fro from the harbour.

On turning round the northern end of the island the rocks were seen to be covered with hundreds of sea birds, Cormorants, Gulls and Oyster Catchers amongst others. They were all quite unperturbed by our little dinghy as JR guided us expertly into the small sandy bay to begin our exploration. On wading ashore the first impression gained was of an overpowering pungent smell, the legacy of the large bird population. We pulled the dinghy high up onto the sand as the tide was coming in and we did not want to lose it and be left stranded. Near where we came ashore the remains of a wreck was protruding through the sand marking out the shape of an ill-fated ship.

We made our way to the natural rocky causeway which joins the North Islet at low tide, hurriedly striding across before the tide cut it off again. Almost immediately we stumbled over a wasps nest on the ground and made an even quicker exit back over the causeway.

We had to tread carefully trying not to step on any of the

numerous dead birds scattered on the ground. Swarms of flies agitated above the corpses. The shore line was littered with dry white bones. This could have been Robinson Crusoe's island with shipwrecks and bones and the only sound being the call of the birds swooping overhead. It was hard to believe that we were only half a mile across the water from home.

We then turned our attention to the tower and made our way towards it stepping over the abandoned nests on the grass, at this time of year all now empty.

What a beautiful safe haven for the birds this island is. The ground covering is very pleasantly carpeted with masses of white marguerette daises with colourful splashes of mauve michaelmas daises sprinkled in their midst. Near the tower were small deep pools of water. At one time they might have been fresh but are now slimy, green and stagnant, surrounded by long grass and nettles.

The tower is very impressive, still standing with no sign of erosion after nearly two hundred years. It must have been an enormous undertaking to build this conspicuous tower. Each huge heavy block of stone had to be transported out to the island and lifted into position. It is truly a magnificent example of fine workmanship. This tower was and still is a prominent warning for all shipping to steer well clear of the dangers around it. As for the unfortunate mariners who came to grief here the tower offered shelter and a chance of survival.

A sturdy flight of nine steps leads up to the doorway ensuring the entrance is always kept above the level of the high tides. Part of the iron brackets where the door hinges were mounted still remain on the doorway but the door is long gone. Inside the floor is thickly covered with compacted

> This could have been Robinson Crusoe's island with shipwrecks and bones and the only sound being the call of the birds swooping overhead

bird droppings built up over the years. Constructed in one corner is a little fireplace with a chimney reaching right up to the top. When a fire was burning the smoke would have been seen emerging from the top of the tower. The tower is square built and the large arched windows on each of the four sides allow a clear view in every direction. The window space is wide enough to sit in while absorbing the splendid views. In the past centuries the shipwrecked seafarers would have been anxiously looking out for any sign of rescue. The tower had originally been divided into three levels and a wall ladder enabled access to be gained to each floor. Unfortunately the dividing wooden floors have at some time been set on fire and burned away.

We three were quite content to sit watching the birds while pondering over the past dramas and tragedies that had taken place on this very spot.

All too soon it was time to leave to catch the tide. On detouring back to the dinghy we noticed lots of coal still scattered around, obviously the lost cargo from some stricken vessel. Could it have come from the coal carrying smack *Welcome*? She had come to grief in 1891 while leaving Ardrossan Harbour fully laden. We even picked up pieces of the blue and white tiles Coralie Campbell mentioned.

As we waded out from the bay, pushing the dinghy, the water was shallow and so crystal clear. Once back aboard our craft we noticed how quickly the water became very deep. The sun was still shining as we bid the island farewell and left it with its many secrets.

The authors